Silence All Round Marked

An Historical Play in Hysteria Writ

Douglas Messerli

A Blue Corner Drama Book: Number 4
A Division of Corner Books

Blue Corner Drama Books
A Division of
Corner Books
6148 Wilshire Boulevard. Los Angeles, California 90048

First Published in paperback in 1991 by Corner Books

10 9 8 7 6 5 4 3 2
FIRST EDITION

Cover: *Park Piece (Tables)*, by Robin Palanker
Reproduced by permission of the artist

LIBRARY OF CONGRESS CATALOGING IN PUBLICATION DATA
Messerli, Douglas (1947)
Silence All Round Marked: An Historical
Play in Hysteria Writ
p. cm — (Blue Corner Drama: 5)
ISBN: 1-55713-125-2
I. Title. II. Series.
811',54—dc19

Printed in the United States of America
by McNaughton & Gunn

Silence All Round Marked
An Historical Play in Hysteria Writ

Other Titles by this Author

River to Rivet: A Poetic Trilogy, 1984
Dinner on the Lawn, 1979, 1982
River to Rivet: A Manifesto, 1984
Some Distance, 1982
Maxims from My Mother's Milk/Hymns to Him: A Dialogue, 1988

Anthologies:

Contemporary American Fiction, 1983
[edited with an Introduction]
''Language'' Poetries: An Anthology, 1987
[edited with an Introduction]

Blue Corner Drama Series

1. *The Professional Frenchman,* Mac Wellman
2. *Bad Penny,* Mac Wellman
3. *Guards of the Heart,* Joe Ross
4. *Silence All Round Marked: An Historical Play in Hysteria Writ,* Douglas Messerli

Forthcoming:

The Tower, Matthew Maguire
Behind the Heart, Sande Zeig
The Crazy Plays, Jeffrey Jones
Gogol, Len Jenkin

Scene 1

*[*JIMMY *walks onto stage, shushing the audience. At the door of a nearby house he knocks. It opens up.]*

JIMMY: Hello?

NORA: Hey!

JIMMY: Is the mistress in?

NORA: I am the mistress!

JIMMY: *[Looks her over]* Is there a daughter then?

NORA: *[Offended she is offhanded with him]* She's not about.

JIMMY: She isn't up?

NORA: She's not in.

JIMMY: She's out? *[Turning to go]* I'll be back.

NORA: *[Jumping upon his shoulders]*

Ride a cock-horse to Banbury Bay
And carry some sugar
And meet him with hay
And he shall lay down
With you and stay!

JIMMY: *[Attempting to disengage]* Get off me! Get off!

NORA: Giddy up! Giddy up!

JIMMY: Get off! What are you doing? Get off!

NORA: *[Getting more excited every second]* Giddy, up! Giddy, up!

JIMMY: *[Finally throwing her, she falls with a crack]* What on earth was that all for?

NORA: *[With great difficulty, sitting up]* I like you!

JIMMY: That ain't the way to my heart!

NORA: I was after your netherpart, your little dart—not your bleeding beating box!

JIMMY: You're Irish! That's it. You're an Irish wife!

NORA: I?

JIMMY: Mistresses generally are, right?

NORA: The red-head ones are. Sometimes. But blondes *[fluffing up her obviously peroxided hair]* are empty-headed sluts.

JIMMY: But you've got red hair!

NORA: Where?

JIMMY: *[Pointing to her eyebrows]* There!

NORA: That's not fair! I can't dye...my eye...

JIMMY: *[Bows]*...You are a Red!

NORA: *[Mocking him]* I admit. I'll even testify!

JIMMY: That explains your obviously bizarre, antisocial insolence. Politics is dangerous stuff.

NORA: It was the foreman Duffy who put it in my head, said you want to get up in the world, get up in the morn with me and see yourself how the workers go to sea. I saw an army of insipid saints. I saw....

JIMMY: A way to get out...of the house, city, state....

NORA: *[Making it up]* I was put in touch...with agents. Americans. The Soviets. They were as sweet as beets in gin.

JIMMY: That's the trouble with all you good people of drear Dublin. Everything starts with potatoes and stops with what you make of them.

NORA: I like you also, as I've said.

JIMMY: I too am fond of myself. That's why I came out.... to see your son.

NORA: *My* sun belongs to everyone.

JIMMY: I want to fly with him in the highest sky...and..... crash back to earth again!

NORA: You English?

JIMMY: No. Greek.

NORA: You don't talk like one. Lebanese?

JIMMY: My father was Plato, Lesbia my mamma. My uncle, Socrates!

NORA: So why did you ask to date my daughter Deidre then?

JIMMY: To be polite.

NORA: Polite?

JIMMY: You know, my bringing up.

NORA: But I don't have a daughter.

JIMMY: You don't?

NORA: Nor a son.

JIMMY: *[Disappointedly]* Well, I've got a long ways to go tonight.

NORA: *[Calling him back]* I have a husband, ten years my junior, though.

JIMMY: Ten years?

NORA: Twenty then!

JIMMY: *[Pondering the implications]* No. No.

NORA: *[Quick]* Twenty-five, I admit. I am the Queen of Innisbrofin.

JIMMY: The what?

NORA: You know, the sirens. The Irish equivalent. I'm one. I drove him down from County Darby straight into the heart...of my mother...and into my arms the very same night.

JIMMY: *[Giving her a look over once more]* You don't look like a siren.

NORA: Look into my eyes.

JIMMY: I don't do that! *[Responding to* NORA'S *confusion]* That also isn't polite. And you never know....

NORA: What you might see there?

JIMMY: If they see you...or someone else.

NORA: Now who could a comely lad like you be thinking they might see instead?

JIMMY: You know, anyone. Anyone! They may see a druggist when you're a whore. Or when you're just a lecturer, a priest!

NORA: *[Amazed at his leaps]* Who? Who am I supposed to see in those blue, blue eyes of yours turned scarlet in your nights of seldom sleep?

JIMMY: Could be a cousin...an aunt...

NORA: A mother?

JIMMY: Perhaps.

NORA: Maybe a father? An uncle? *[*JIMMY *attempts to cover his blanch]* An uncle! *[Jumping onto his shoulders once more]*

Ride a cock-horse to Dorchester bourse
To buy a pat of butter of course.
Take him there and give him some air
And into your ears he'll mutter
Sweet words he'd never utter
To his loving mother.

JIMMY: Get off! Off! You're daffy!

NORA: You've become the psychologically interesting one. *[Frieze and blackout]*

Scene 2

JIMMY: *[In the arms of* NORA*]* Once more.

[She kisses him]

Once again.

[She kisses]

Just a little one.

NORA: *[With finger to her lips]* Shhhhh.

JIMMY: Am I shouting again?

NORA: No. But you were looking like you might....

JIMMY: Oh. Yes. Yes. I was...seeking....

NORA: And you found.

JIMMY: The seven C's.

NORA: Communion, Candor, Circumpsection, Charm, Creation, Constancy, and...Capital!

JIMMY: You—you are a bitch!

NORA: You want my money or not?

JIMMY: I want...want to live a life pure...

NORA: As a driven plow.

JIMMY: I want...

*[*NORA *kisses him once more.]*

JIMMY: *[Standing]* Get away from me!

NORA: Just because I see through you, see through the fool you want to be but can't.

JIMMY: I think you revealed yourself.

NORA: Never! I don't trust any man enough!

JIMMY: Just jump 'em. Don't rely on their support?

NORA: Oh, I trust in their thighs, in their sighs, their lust. I just don't rely on what's in their eyes.

JIMMY: Don't insinuate.

NORA: I? They're, like my hair, fellow travellers of where we're taken in.

JIMMY: I'm no sympathizer!

NORA: No, you're just the enemy!

JIMMY: *[Putting his finger to mouth]* Shhhh! This is too early in the plot.

NORA: I apologize. I couldn't resist. May I kiss you again?

JIMMY: You better not.

NORA: Come on, just a little one!

JIMMY: When's your son due?

NORA: *[Patting her pregnant stomach]* In about two minutes.

JIMMY: And what, in the meantime, are we going to do to...*[gesturing to the audience]* entertain.

NORA: *[Marching up the apron and peering out]* With them!

JIMMY: *[Pulling her back]* Now that really makes for a relationship. Them! They're us. At least pretend.

NORA: What for? We're here for a reason, aren't we? We're actors. We make the meaning. We are the play. While they, they can only watch. *[Mocking the audience]*

JIMMY: That's where you're out of touch. They make the play. We but strut....We perform what they create.

NORA: *[Kissing him quick]* Do they get to do that? No, they can only stay in their seats. They can't kiss the person sitting next to them—even if they wanted to—without causing a stir and fuss. They can only desire...to be here...kissing your lips. While I can do....anything...*[beginning to strip]*, even rip the blousssse ...away and whip off the dresssssss—under

duresssssss and *[in panties and bra she begins a gritty soft shoe]* dance!
[Frieze and blackout]

Scene 3

JIMMY: *[Staring into his lap.]* Bugabugabugaboo! Abugabugabugabugger. Abugabuggerbugaboo!

BOTH: *[Putting their fingers to mouths]* Shhhhhh!

JIMMY: He's sleeping.

NORA: *[To audience]* She sleeps.

JIMMY: Cute as a bug.

NORA: She'll be a pin-up.

JIMMY: He'll be in all the male magazines.

NORA: *[To audience]* As you see, there is some confusion.

JIMMY: Bugabugabuga.

NORA: I ask you.

JIMMY: Bugaboo. Bugaboo.

NORA: To involve yourselves. Come. Come on up! See a real true little babe, fresh from the oven!

And the audience comes, one by one, onto the stage, some immediately overcome, in tears, others merely peering into the lap of JIMMY *to witness what lies there before them.*

JIMMY: You judge. What sex is this infant? *[Holding up a doll]*

Part of the audience shouts "male," others "female," while others keep silent with their doubts.

JIMMY: There's no question. The males have it.

NORA: I think the females won.

JIMMY: Bugabuggerbooybooboo.

NORA: You see this maniac. This is what I have to live with day and night. You can go home after this play. I have to stay. Clean up. Put away the dishes, chairs, tables,and all the other props. He keeps the baby away from me until he drops asleep so I have to hold the crying child and feed and diaper her and speak to her normally. Otherwise...she'll grow up to be someone who loves a man...like him. A pervert!

JIMMY: Shhhhhh! He's asleep.

NORA: She's...so beautiful though...and worth all the suffering.

*[*JIMMY *falls asleep, and* NORA *takes the child away.]*

[A loudspeaker cries like a baby, and NORA *walks the infant up and down.]*

NORA: If you're going to be a woman free you've got to disagree with everyone...except your sisters. They can be trusted to a certain point in time and space, until they will try to drag you into the bushes too. And then you'll know, it may already be too late! You have to act immediately! Get a knife......

As she speaks, she continues to walk the child up and down stage. Returning from backstage she suddenly appears without the baby, flourishing instead a large black scarf and magician's stick, pulling away the scarf.

The CHILD *has become a teenager, a boy in a woman's wig or a girl with hair severly cut.]*

...and free their hearts from their bosoms. Drape them—carefully—across the trellis in full moonlight. Take the hand of the man who wants you very much and stroll, slowly, very slowly, with your hand in his, promising—if you must—to kiss him if he'll stand under this trellis for a minute. The blood, you see, will seep into his hair and from there into his head and, gradually, after several months throughout his entire system, vital organs, disgestive juices, enzymes, proteins, corpuscles and such, until, transformed, he'll come to you as the sister might—had she had the opportunity—gently as a rabbit in mad heat! You won't even know he's been there when he's gone.

CHILD: Will I have any memory?

NORA: None.

CHILD: And what if I want him back?

NORA: *[Producing a large magician's hat]* Just draw him out of the hat. *She pulls* JIMMY *from the hat, who in the process is awakened.*

[Frieze and blackout]

Scene 4

[Seeing the CHILD, JIMMY *begins to salivate.]*

JIMMY: Woman, you lie. You said you didn't have a son!

NORA: I said I had a daughter.

JIMMY: And you didn't have one!

NORA: I was open-minded.

JIMMY: You didn't have a husband!

NORA: No. But that was, even then, all in the past. The future, where now we live, was uncurling even as I spoke. I had a daughter but I didn't. I had a husband who was much younger to whom I wasn't married yet. So what else could the truth have been? I did and didn't. I didn't and I did.

JIMMY: You're the most slippery, slimey little hellgrammite on this planet!

NORA: I hate you too. But it won't do to argue before our baby as if she had to be the judge.

JIMMY: I agree. Come here, Peter. Come, sit on my lap.

NORA: *[To the* CHILD*]* You be careful now. *[To* JIMMY*]* You be careful.

JIMMY: Let me tell you a story or two.....

NORA: *[Leaving the room, but not without once or twice turning back]* You both behave yourselves.

JIMMY: Once upon a time there was a man...who was a magician of sorts...

CHILD: Like mommy?

JIMMY: *[A bit confused]* No. No. A real magician. A sorcerer. A wizard. A THAUMATURGE!

CHILD: Who?

JIMMY: A maker of miracles, wonderments. Now this man could do many things. Change brass into gold. Emeralds to diamonds. Diamonds to...an entire mountain range. But there was one thing very special —more wondrous than all of these—he could accomplish best. He could fly. Not just in an aeroplane or by stradling some bird's back, but all by himself. *[*JIMMY*, standing from the beginning of this tale, suddenly produces a huge pair of wings]* With wings—these wonderful wings—he'd woven from an eagle or two and the eye of a newt and an old mistress's hairdo. And when he flew it was better than the smell of lilacs through windows, better than when the wind rides through hair like a Brahma Bull on the buck, better still than the way you will feel when you first fuck. He flew so high, he had several orgasms before he could even say "holy cow." *[The* CHILD *laughs]*.

So everyday, day after day, out he flew on a soar, hardly able to control his breath. Day after day life was as good as it gets.

But then one night, he thought, I'd like to share this with someone. Someone I love as much as my flight. My son perhaps. And so he went back into his lab in the old labyrinth and built another pair of wings, more sturdy, more durable, and even more beautiful than the first set.

When he told his son of the special treat he had in store, the boy was so excited, he got terribly impatient.

He ran straight to the lab and placed wings across his back. And flapped! And flapped! And rose right through the ceiling, above the town-hall spire, the clouds, the stratosphere, and clear out of gravity. Rising still higher and higher and higher he started toward the sun. And the father flew, as quickly as he could, after. But he was a little old and couldn't flap as fast. He called out, ''Be careful. Don't get too close!''

But the son was so far ahead he could hardly hear what his father said. And he was so filled with pleasure he couldn't control himself. He flew too near the inferno and his wings caught fire, which sent him precipitously into a spin, and the boy began to drop and drop and drop and drop, right into the arms of his father who, holding him, couldn't continue the motion of his wings, couldn't keep them in the sky aloft. And so together they fell, heads hurled down straight into the ground.

The CHILD *is clearly terrified by the story.*

JIMMY: *[Holding open his wings]* Come in. *[As the* CHILD *clings to him,* JIMMY *enfolds him in his wings.]*

NORA *appears stage left, suitcases in hand, quite obviously still pregnant.*

NORA: Put your boy and toys away. The time has come.

[Frieze and blackout]

Scene 5

NURSE: *[Dressed in a nun's habit]* Shhhhh! She's sleeping.

JIMMY: Is she okay?

NURSE: Of course. And fine lass too with head of red.

JIMMY: And my wife?

NURSE: Don't know.

JIMMY: And the other one?

NURSE: You mean the metaphor?

JIMMY: What?

NURSE: The metaphor.

JIMMY: No! I mean my son.

NURSE: The metaphor.

JIMMY: The living, breathing babe born in my breeches and killed—if you're trying to tell me what I think—by my breach.

NURSE: The metaphor.

JIMMY: Is that what she says?

NURSE: She's still comatose.

JIMMY: So out with it! What do you mean?

NURSE: Sir, I don't mean....As a nurse I just report.

[She exits]

JIMMY: This is all getting to be a bore. *[To audience]* You poor people might as well go home...if she's right. Goodnight! If I have spent these last fifteen minutes and one half with a figure of speech, beware. I haven't begun to fight.

She lies like a lizard, there in her bed, her head stuck out in sinful pride. Who's the father, I'd like to

know. And why did she try to hide? And why didn't she get a decent abortion instead?
And where is the sun I so loved?
[Frieze. Complete blackout.]

Scene 6

NORA: *[Completely in the dark]* Am I dead? Is this the grave? The grief forgiven. The long arm of love reached out to never never touch. I think I hear him overhead. He's crying, not so much for me—yet more than he thinks—but for the son I should have had instead.

I remember that first day, he came to me, a childish crusader on his way to confusion instead of a quest, asking after my mother, my father, my brother, even my aunt. Pretending he was more interested in all of them than in me.

And I was oh so shy. Hysterically. Whispering in the shadows "hello" and "goodbye" as if there were nothing to be said for the hours in-between.

Together we have seen so many things. Imagined more. Hoped for much too much. Desired less. That is the secret blessing of love, even if dressed in hate. I wanted to tell him that. But now it is too late.

[Frieze. Lights snap on.]

Scene 7

JIMMY: *[Calling at his own house]* Come out! Come out Miranda and play!

NORA: *[Leaning from the upper window]* Shhh—shush your caterwauling mouth!

JIMMY: Let your daughter out and I won't shout.

NORA: She's busy with dishes, floors, corners filled with cobwebs, and rugs, rugs, rugs!

JIMMY: Send her out! Send her out!

NORA: You be quiet or I'll...

MIRANDA: *[Suddenly at the door]* Here I am old dad. Here. Now what's getting you all so worked up?

JIMMY: *[Gesturing to his daughter to come closer]* I've got something.

MIRANDA: *[Loudly]* Something?

JIMMY: Shhhhh. Something. But tell me first, do you love me more?

MIRANDA: More than who?

JIMMY: Than yourself, my dear.

MIRANDA: You, mother—no, John Patrick Henry Howe!

JIMMY: And who'll he be now?

MIRANDA: You sound like an old hoot! You know very well and it won't help if you pout.

JIMMY: Who is this J P Henry? Who's he?

MIRANDA: The man I'm going to marry.

JIMMY: I thought you always said that was me.

MIRANDA: At first perhaps.

JIMMY: More recently!

MIRANDA: And at twelve. But now it's getting late. *[She begins to head in]*

JIMMY: I've got something!

NORA: *[Appearing at the window again]* You've got a sick head!

JIMMY: Shoosh woman! Get yourself in! *[Signalling for his daughter to join him]* Over here.

MIRANDA: *[Finally a little bit curious]* What is it? A bush?

JIMMY: That's weeds.

MIRANDA: A hat?

JIMMY: A rock that is, not for your head unless you want it cracked.

MIRANDA: So tell me, tell me.

JIMMY: *[From behind the rock he pulls out an enormously large set of wings.] [Beaming]* See!

MIRANDA: What is that?

JIMMY: *[Putting them on]* It isn't a that! It's things. Wings for you to fly away as far as your heart contents to be.

MIRANDA: Now what would I want to do that for?

JIMMY: To fly, of course! To get high. Higher than anyone else. To escape on a breeze!

MIRANDA: And where's Mister John Patrick Henry going to be when I'm winging my way to some or another oak tree? You're daft!

JIMMY: Am not. They fly. They fly! They work, believe me!

MIRANDA: I've got to go scrub. *[Heads back to the house]*

JIMMY: No. No! These are real! They're actual wings! See!

He flaps the wings and goes nowhere fast as she turns back.

MIRANDA: *[Clapping in mockery]* Hurray! Hurray! Now go play with yourself.

[She exits into the house.]
Jimmy stands for a moment in utter confusion, dispirited.

Again he flaps, and this time begins a slow rise. Flaps more and disappears out of sight.
[Blackout]

Scene 8

Evening light. There are dinner tables in the yard, formally set with festoons, paper, white, the remainders of a wedding fest. A young man sits impatiently waiting at one of the tables, tapping his fingers, his feet. Suddenly Miranda appears at the door in a white frock as pure as she pretends to be. The young man rises in more ways than one.

JPH HOWE: Yes...you're...

MIRANDA: A vision?

JPH HOWE: More!

MIRANDA: *[Mocking him]* A whole landscape then?

JPH HOWE: Yes! *[Realizing his mistake]* Well, more like a dell. A little shaded glen.

MIRANDA: You talk such claptrap.

JPH HOWE: It's love, of course!

MIRANDA: It's not so course. Just claptrap. If father were here....

JPH HOWE: Your father! I'm your husband. I'm now the man of the house!

MIRANDA: Some man. I wonder where he could have got?

JPH HOWE: He was a strange one alright. A real genius they all say.

MIRANDA: A homosexual genius!

JPH HOWE: A what?

MIRANDA: I think that's why we got along so well. He really wanted a son, and sometimes, I think, he saw me as one.

JPH HOWE: Well, I'll never see you...

MIRANDA: I know dear.

JPH HOWE: ...as anything but the beautiful princess...

MIRANDA: I know dear.

JPH HOWE: ...you've always been.

MIRANDA: That's why I miss him. He was truly mad.

JPH HOWE: I'll take you away from all that!

MIRANDA: No, I'll make you mad before the end of the night!

NORA: *[Running out of the house]* Now, you two give a kiss and I'll toss some potatoes at you!

MIRANDA: *[Hugging her mother]* I'll miss you too.

NORA: No. That's the wonder of it.

JPH HOWE: The wonder?

NORA: *[Rolling her eyes]* The wonder. The miracle of two people who can't keep their hands to themselves.

[JPH HOWE looks perplexed]

MIRANDA: Come on John P H Howe. It's time to go now.

[JPH HOWE bows to his mother-in-law]

[The couple exit quickly]

[At the very moment of their disappearance JIMMY falls from the skies.]

JIMMY: Owwww!

NORA: Serves you right!

JIMMY: Owwww! Owwww! Owwww!

NORA: If I had some nails this minute I'd drive them right through your heart!

JIMMY: *[Looking about]* What's going on here?

NORA: It's gone, all gone, my dear.

JIMMY: Who? What? Owwww!

NORA: *[Coming over to him and tenderly putting his head into her lap]* So you decided to come back.

JIMMY: I fell.

NORA: You fell?

JIMMY: Lost my wings.

NORA: Now who could have cut them?

JIMMY: They just fell.

NORA: Well, then it was meant.

JIMMY: She marry that priggish little bluebonnet man?

NORA: That she did.

JIMMY: I couldn't stand to see the disgrace.

NORA: She'll whip him up right.

JIMMY: I'm lonely.

NORA: You've still got me.

JIMMY: *[Lifting his head for a moment, she pushes it back and elbows it into a lock]* I'm lonely!

NORA: Hush. You're just tired. Hush.

JIMMY: I'm lonely. Confused.

NORA: Shhhh now. Be still.

JIMMY: *[Struggling to sit up]* There are times, have been, times, whole episodes of my life, leap past my mind. And I think I've lived a scene I never did or couldn't have or oughtn't to.

NORA: I know.

JIMMY: And I don't remember things they go so fast. Or when I do, they seem to never happen the way they were supposed to or even the way they really did.

NORA: I know.

JIMMY: I thought I was going to be somebody else. Somebody strange and brave when I was young.

NORA: You were.

JIMMY: But I seemed to turn out just about like everyone else.

NORA: That's growing up.

JIMMY: *[Again lying down with his head in her lap]* No, that's death. It's death does that.

NORA: Shhhhh now.

JIMMY: I really did fly, you know. For a while I did.

NORA: Hush.

[Blackout]